GENOCIDE IN MODERN TIMES™

THE ARMENIAN GENOCIDE

Jeri Freedman

ROSEN
PUBLISHING®

New York

Published in 2009 by The Rosen Publishing Group, Inc.
29 East 21st Street, New York, NY 10010
www.rosenpublishing.com

Library of Congress Cataloging-in-Publication Data

Freedman, Jeri.
The Armenian genocide / Jeri Freedman. — 1st ed.
    p. cm.
ISBN-13: 978-1-4042-1825-3 (library binding)
1. Armenian massacres, 1915–1923. 2. Armenians—Turkey—History.
I. Title.
DS195.5.F745 2008
956.6'20154—dc22

                                                    2007044917

Manufactured in the United States of America

On the cover: *Foreground:* People pay their respects to victims of the
Armenian genocide at a memorial in the Armenian capital, Yerevan.

CONTENTS

INTRODUCTION

The term "genocide" was first used in 1943 by Jewish legal scholar Raphael Lemkin. It is a combination of two terms: *genos*, which is Greek for tribe or race, and *cide*, which means "killing." Genocide is the deliberate killing of a group of people who are of the same ethnic, religious, or national background. A key factor in genocide is that it is deliberate, or planned. The intention is to destroy all the people in a particular group. The Armenian genocide was planned by government officials in Turkey, the center of the Ottoman Empire. The genocide was carried out between 1915 and 1917, during World War I. The victims were ethnic Armenians living in Turkey. Estimates of how many Armenians were killed range from hundreds of thousands to 1.5 million. Some Armenians were killed directly. Others died when large groups of them were marched long distances from their native villages. During the marches, they had little food

In 2005, an estimated eight thousand people gathered in Times Square in New York City to honor the Armenians killed in the genocide. The date marked the ninetieth anniversary of the beginning of the genocide, in 1915.

and few supplies. In addition, they faced attacks from both Turks and Kurds, a tribal people who lived within the lands of the Ottoman Empire.

This book provides historical background on the events that led to the Armenian genocide. It then explains what happened during the genocide and in its aftermath. Finally, it takes a closer look at how this period in Armenian history is viewed today.

1

Historical Background

Armenians have lived in northeastern Turkey since ancient times. They are a distinct ethnic group that originated in the Caucasus, an area bordered on the southwest by Turkey and on the north by Russia. Armenians have their own language and their own culture, including music and dance. Christianity is the traditional Armenian religion. The earliest Armenian Christian churches date back to the first century CE. Armenia is recognized as the first country to adopt Christianity as its official religion, in 301 CE.

The center of the Armenian homeland is the base of Mt. Ararat, a large mountain in northeastern Turkey. Armenia was much larger than it is today. It extended from what is now known as the Republic of Armenia and Azerbaijan south to the Iraq and Iran borders. The country sits in a strategic position. For this reason, it has been invaded many times. At different times in its history, Armenia was occupied by Assyrians, Greeks, Romans, Persians, Mongols, and Turks, among others.

In 1071, Armenia was conquered by the Turks, an ethnic group living to the west. The majority of Turks are Muslims. Hence, religion was a source of conflict for many years before the Armenian genocide occurred. By the 1100s, the Turkish Empire weakened and

Armenian women weave a rug in a Chicago storefront in 1919. By putting their traditional skills on display, the women raised funds to help starving people back in Armenia.

the Armenians were able to establish an independent state again. However, from the 1200s to the 1400s, Armenia was repeatedly invaded by the Mongols, Asian tribes united under warlord Genghis Khan (c. 1162–1227). In the 1500s, a weakened Armenia was divided up between the Turks of the Ottoman Empire and the Persian Empire, centered in present-day northwest Iran. The eastern, Persian part of Armenia was later conquered by Russia, becoming part of the Russian Empire.

THE OTTOMAN EMPIRE

At the time of the Armenian genocide, Turkey was only part of the land controlled by the Turks. Beginning in 1299, the Turks conquered a large part of Europe, Asia, and North Africa. In addition to present-day Turkey and Armenia, the areas controlled by the Turks included parts of Macedonia, Slovakia, Hungary, Serbia, Romania, Ukraine, Iraq, Saudi Arabia, Israel, Egypt, and Algeria. Altogether, more than thirty countries were once part of this sprawling empire. The first ruler of this empire was Osman I; therefore, it is called the Ottoman Empire after him. The Ottoman Empire lasted for more than six hundred years, from 1299 until 1922. It lasted so long, in part, because its leaders tolerated different ethnic groups living within its borders, as long as they were peaceful. The empire was broken up following the Ottoman defeat in World War I.

ARMENIANS IN THE OTTOMAN EMPIRE

Turks ruled the area that had been Armenia from the sixteenth century until the end of World War I. Like much of the world's population during this time, Armenians were mostly farmers. However, they were also active in business, and many held important positions such as bankers and merchants. Being Christians, Armenians in the Muslim Ottoman Empire were never trusted by the authorities. The distrust between the groups dated back many years. During the Middle Ages, for example, the Catholic Church mounted numerous military crusades into the region south of Turkey. Their purpose was to recapture the holy city of Jerusalem, which had fallen under Muslim control. The series of bloody battles left lasting bad feelings between Christians and Muslims.

For the right to live in the Muslim Ottoman Empire, Armenians had to pay special taxes. They were not allowed to testify in court or to bear arms. In addition, they had to pay bribes to local Turkish officials to be allowed to live and work in safety. Armenians also faced opposition from the Kurds, a group living throughout the region to the south and east of Turkey. Despite the bribes Armenians paid, the villages where they lived were often attacked by local Turks and Kurdish tribesmen.

THE REIGN OF SULTAN ABDUL HAMID II

In 1876, Abdul Hamid II (1870–1909) became sultan (king) of the Ottoman Empire. He was a harsh ruler with absolute power. During his reign, the conflict between Armenians and Turks in the Ottoman Empire came to a head.

The Armenian Question

In 1877, Russia went to war with the Ottoman Empire. The Russians wanted to capture parts of the empire, including the areas that are now Bulgaria, Romania, Montenegro, and Serbia. One of Russia's main goals was to capture the territory known as the Balkan Peninsula, as this would gain Russia access to the Mediterranean Sea for trade and military transport. Early in 1878, Russia accepted a truce offer from the Ottoman leaders and signed the Treaty of San Stefano. Under the treaty, the Ottoman Empire ceded key areas of the Balkan Peninsula to Russia.

The great western European powers were alarmed by Russia's success in expanding its influence into eastern Europe. Acting together, England, France, Austria-Hungary, Germany, and Italy forced the Russians to accept changes to the Treaty of San Stefano. As a result, Serbia, Romania, and Montenegro became independent countries, and part of Bulgaria was returned to the Ottoman Empire. The new agreement they drew up is known as the Treaty of Berlin.

The Russians had long claimed to be the protectors of Christian Armenians, and during the war, Armenia was one of the places where the Russians stationed troops. Sultan Abdul Hamid II resented the Armenian support of the Russians. Fearing that he would take vengeance on the Armenians, European leaders debated the best way to protect the Armenians. This was known as "the Armenian question." In the end, the European powers never came up with a good answer to the question.

Sultan Abdul Hamid II, the thirty-fourth sultan of the Ottoman Empire, is shown here dressed in his military uniform. He was called the Great Assassin by those who opposed his policies.

The Hamidian Armenian Massacres

By 1890, Armenians were becoming fearful and restless with their situation. They began to demand the protections the Ottoman government had agreed to in the Treaty of Berlin. They wanted to be treated equally with Muslims in courts of law, and they wanted to bring an end to the unfair taxation and discrimination that they had put up with. At the same time, Armenians began to express a greater sense of Armenian nationalism, a pride in or devotion to their own ethnic group. In case of armed confrontation with the Turks, Armenian nationalists were being armed by the newly founded Armenian Revolutionary Federation.

Armenians' demands for change were spurred by an increase in education. In the late nineteenth century, many schools had been set up by the Armenian Apostolic Church, to which most Armenians belonged. Also in the nineteenth century, Protestant missionaries from America arrived in Armenia and began exposing Armenians to the American social ideals of liberty and equality. These ideas appealed greatly to the Armenians, who were treated as second-class citizens in the Ottoman Empire.

The first armed clash between Armenian nationalists and Ottoman forces took place in 1894, in Sasun, in northern Turkey. When Armenians there refused to pay their taxes, the Ottoman government sent in Turkish and Kurdish soldiers, who easily defeated the overmatched Armenians.

From 1894 to 1896, constant attacks against Armenians were carried out by Kurds armed by the Ottoman government. These actions were designed to keep the Armenians in line and to discourage them from attempting to adopt the European and American ideas of equality and freedom. Armenians' property and businesses were taken from them, and dozens of villages were burned. Between 100,000 and 300,000 Armenians were killed, and thousands more fled the country. This series of atrocities (monstrous acts) is known as the Hamidian massacres.

This drawing is from an English newspaper printed in 1896. It shows members of the Turkish Red Cross Society carrying away the dead after a massacre of Armenians in Constantinople (now Istanbul).

The Young Turks

In response to the oppressive policies of Sultan Abdul Hamid II, several reform-minded Turkish groups had come together back in 1889. They became known as the Young Turks. By 1906, the Young Turks had formed a political party called the Committee of Union and Progress (CUP). The CUP forced the sultan from the throne and established a parliament with elected representatives. Initially, the parliament included non-Muslim minorities, such as Jews and Armenians. Before long, however, pro-Muslim elements among the Young Turks rose to take control of the party.

CONFLICT IN THE EMPIRE

By the start of the twentieth century, the Ottoman Empire was coming apart, as Bulgaria, Bosnia-Herzegovina, and Albania gained their independence. As the empire unraveled, Muslim hatred toward Armenian Christians grew. Because of schools and colleges funded by missionaries, many Armenians were better educated than their Turkish neighbors. As a result, they tended to have better-paying jobs in business and trade than many Turks. In 1909, yet another massacre took place, this one in southern Turkey. Armenians in Adana and nearby villages were attacked, with as many as thirty thousand Armenians dying. The cause of the massacre is unclear, but one factor was the rising tide of Turkish Muslim nationalism, fostered by the CUP. A new source of stress was about to be added to the already explosive situation: war had come to Europe, and Turkey was about to become involved.

2

The Turks at War

The fighting of World War I took place between 1914 and 1918. On June 28, 1914, a Bosnian Serb student shot the heir to the throne of Austria-Hungary. In response, Austria-Hungary attacked Serbia. All of the major nations and states in Europe had treaties with other European nations. Therefore, once one country attacked another, they were all obliged to provide military support to one side or the other. Shortly, all of the major European powers were divided into two groups: the Central Powers on one side, and the Entente Powers, or Allies, on the other. (*Entente* is French for "agreement.") The Central Powers included the German states, Bulgaria, Austria-Hungary, and nations that were part of their empires. The Entente Powers included France, Britain, Russia, the Italian states, and nations that were part of their empires. At the outset, the United States was a neutral country. (However, the United States joined the Entente Powers in 1917.)

Early in 1914, Turkey and Germany had signed a treaty agreeing to provide military support to each other. So, when the war started, Turkey joined the Central Powers fighting against the Entente Powers.

THE CAMPAIGN IN ARMENIA

Ismail Enver, or Enver Pasha, was one of the Young Turks. ("Pasha" is a title used by high officials in Turkey.) In 1914, he was minister of war for the Ottoman Empire. When Turkey entered World War I, Enver Pasha decided to try to take back the Armenian lands lost to the Russians in the Russo-Turkish War of 1877–1878. On December 22, he sent troops into the Russian-occupied lands, but his army was soundly defeated. Tens of thousands of Turkish troops were killed in battle, and many more died in the harsh winter retreat. There is evidence that the bad weather and inadequate preparation by the Turks played a major role in their defeat. Enver Pasha, however, blamed the Armenians for the loss, claiming they supported the Russians against the Turks.

This engraving from the late nineteenth century shows the Russian Cossack Imperial Guard. They are leading the advance into Turkey during the Russo-Turkish War of 1877–1878.

THE ROLE OF ARMENIA

Against all odds, the Armenians in Turkey tried to remain neutral in World War I. But most Armenians in the Ottoman Empire lived near the border with Russia, the Ottoman enemy. This gave the Turkish government the idea of using the Ottoman Armenians to undermine Russia. Shortly after entering World War I, the Ottoman Turkish government asked Armenians to engage in secret operations across the border in Russia. As a reward for their service, the Armenians would be given additional territory from Russia after its defeat.

For the Turkish Armenians, however, this meant that they would have to attack other Armenians, people of the same ethnic stock and culture. Naturally, the Armenians refused to cooperate. This angered the Ottoman government, which accused Turkish Armenians of being traitors and siding with the Russian enemy. It didn't stop the government from forcing Armenians to fight for the empire, however, as 250,000 Armenian men were impressed into the Ottoman army.

In 1914, the Ottoman government began spreading propaganda, or false information, about the Armenians within the empire. The government claimed that the Armenians were in league with the Russians and that they were a

Ismail Enver (Enver Pasha) is pictured at right. Born into a wealthy family, he studied at military schools and served as an officer in the army prior to becoming the Ottoman Empire's minister of war.

threat to the country's security. In light of this propaganda, World War I provided the Ottoman government with the perfect opportunity to rid itself of the Armenian Christians whose presence in the empire had bothered it for so long.

In 1915, the government issued an order stating that Armenian Christians had to be eliminated. If any Muslim was caught helping Christians, then his or her house would be burned. Then the Muslim, the Muslim's family, and the Christians under the Muslim's protection would all be killed.

KEY FIGURES IN THE GENOCIDE

Enver Pasha, Mehmed Talat, and Ahmed Djemal were the three men who headed the Committee of Union and Progress (CUP). They ran the Ottoman administration during World War I and planned the Armenian genocide. Enver Pasha, minister of war, organized the Teskilati Mahsusa (Special Organization) involved in the Armenian deportations. Mehmed Talat, often referred to by the official title Bey, was secretary general of the CUP. Talat Bey was the individual who ordered the extermination of the Armenians in the Ottoman Empire. Ahmed Djemal was the third major figure in the planning and execution of the genocide. During the war, he governed Syria, a country bordering Turkey to the south. Djemal's rule was so brutal that the citizens of the area eventually revolted.

The activities of government officials weren't limited to eliminating the Armenians. Some were also war profiteers. War profiteers are people who make large amounts of money from selling scarce supplies during a war. According to a September 14, 1915, article in the *New York Times*, "The inhabitants of Constantinople [the Ottoman capital in Turkey, now called Istanbul] are suffering greater hardships than is necessary, because the Committee for National Defense, run by Enver Pasha, Minister of War, and Talat Bey, Minister of the Interior, has cornered all commodities and is selling them at high prices."

Mehmed Talat (Talat Bey), minister of internal affairs in the Ottoman Empire, is generally considered the master planner behind the deportation and massacre of Armenians in the empire.

THE TESKILATI MAHSUSA

The Teskilati Mahsusa, often translated as "Special Organization," was established by the Ottoman government early in the twentieth century. In 1913, it was placed under the control of the war department and Enver Pasha. An organization similar to a secret police force, the Teskilati Mahsusa identified and put an end to antigovernment activities in the Ottoman Empire. Within the Teskilati Mahsusa, many highly skilled soldiers were trained as special-forces troops. During World War I, they engaged in military operations that were too secret or dangerous for regular soldiers.

The Teskilati Mahsusa was employed to suppress the activities of Armenians, whom the government accused of supporting the Russian enemy. Aided by the Teskilati Mahsusa, groups of Kurdish tribesmen and criminals released from prisons attacked and killed many in the caravans of Armenian deportees.

3

Destruction of the Armenian People

In 1915, Mehmed Talat issued a statement accusing the Armenians of attempting to destroy the peace and security of the Ottoman state. This, according to the government, was a threat to the safety and interests of all Turks. Talat went on to accuse the Armenians of joining with the enemies of the Ottoman Empire. Therefore, the government was compelled to take extraordinary measures to preserve the order and security of the country and to promote the welfare of the Armenian community. Armenians, the statement said, were going to be sent away from their communities to places in the interior of the country. This was the official explanation of the government's actions. However, as would soon be revealed, Talat's real goal was to destroy the Armenians in the Ottoman Empire once and for all.

In April 1915, preparations for the deportations began. Armenian men in the Turkish army had their weapons taken away from them and were relieved of their duties. Others were dismissed from government positions. Armenian churches were burned and desecrated, and Armenian schools were forced to close. Teachers, writers, and businessmen were rounded up and taken away. Most of them never returned. On April 24, a large number of Armenian leaders and intellectuals were executed. April 24 is now observed by many Armenians as a day of mourning, in memory of the genocide.

LEGALIZING DEPORTATION

In May 1915, the Ottoman government passed the Temporary Law of Deportation. This gave the government legal authority to deport Armenians at will, simply by declaring them to be suspected of treason. The key element of this law is that it only required suspicion of treason, not proof, to deport someone.

Throughout the empire, orders were sent to police, who began rounding up Armenians. Young men were impressed into the army and

Marchers honor the memory of Armenians killed in the genocide. As of 2004, there were about twenty thousand survivors of the genocide worldwide, the vast majority living outside of Armenia.

sent to the front lines. Older men were forced to work in labor battalions. They were sent to build roads, carry equipment, and do other labor for the war effort. Poorly fed, these men were worked until they dropped from exhaustion.

In a government proclamation from June 1915, Talat issued a list of rules that Armenians had to follow. Eleanor Franklin Egan, an American journalist, wrote these down in the margins of a book and smuggled it out of the country. She reproduced the proclamation in an article that appeared in the February 5, 1916, issue of the *Saturday Evening Post* magazine. The rules stated:

- All Armenians except the sick had to leave their homes within five days, under escort by armed guards.
- Armenians were forbidden from selling their property or lands they owned.
- They were only allowed to take what they could carry.
- If they refused to cooperate, they would be forced to go or be killed.

Armenian deportees were promised protection on the trip, but this turned out to be a lie. Once the Armenians were removed, all of their property was seized by local Turks and any money they kept in banks was taken by the government.

MARCH INTO OBLIVION

Even the elderly, women, and children were marched away from their homes. Those who were not butchered or shot were deported south to the deserts of Mesopotamia (now Iraq) and Syria. They walked as far as the cities of Aleppo, in Syria, and Baghdad, in central Iraq. For huge numbers of Armenians, the "relocation" turned out to be a series of death marches. They were forced to walk day after day without food or

Many Armenians fled Turkey with whatever household goods they could carry away. Above, refugees arrive at the Near East Relief quarters in Alexandropol (now Gyumri) in northwest Armenia.

water. In addition they were attacked by Kurdish tribesmen, who killed many and took what meager possessions they had left. Armenian men traveling with the caravans were usually killed. Young women were often raped or taken captive by Turkish troops or Kurdish tribesmen. The majority of those forced to march from their villages were killed in attacks or died of exposure, exhaustion, or starvation. A 1915 letter from a witness in Turkey stated:

> The exiles will have to traverse on foot a distance that involves one or two months' marching, and sometimes even more, before they reach the particular corner of the desert assigned to them for their

habitation, and destined to become their tomb. We hear, in fact, that the course of their route and the stream of the Euphrates are littered with the corpses of exiles, while those who survive are doomed to certain death, since they will find in the desert neither house, nor work, nor food.

It is simply a scheme for exterminating the Armenian nation wholesale, without any fuss. It is just another form of massacre, and a more horrible form.

In addition, thousands of Armenians in the northern part of Turkey were loaded onto cattle cars and taken by rail to their death. Progress was slow because there was a lot of rail traffic. The trains were needed to move troops and supplies to the battlefront as well. Deportees were often left to wait without food or shelter for days or weeks when the line was backed up, or when the train was needed for other purposes. Even worse, the rail line stopped entirely at two passes in the Tarsus and Amanas mountains. Deportees, often shoeless, then had to get off the train and cross the mountain passes on foot. Because of constant delays, concentration camps were established along these passes, with refugees detained for months in horrible conditions.

In 1915, Christian German missionaries wrote to the German government, an ally of the Turks, asking the government to stop the Turkish deportations of Armenians. The missionaries stated that workers on the Baghdad Railway were not allowed to photograph the deportees as a means to prevent evidence of the atrocities from leaking out. Those who failed to turn over photographs would be arrested and prosecuted by the War Department. The missionaries themselves were forbidden to give food or help to the starving refugees. If they disobeyed, they were arrested.

Henry Wood was a United Press correspondent stationed in the Turkish capital, Constantinople. In an article published August 14, 1915, he reported:

Henry Morgenthau Sr. was the U.S. ambassador to the Ottoman Empire at the time of the Armenian genocide. He later wrote a book about his experiences, titled *Ambassador Morgenthau's Story*.

So critical is the situation that Ambassador Morgenthau [the U.S. ambassador to Turkey], who alone is fighting to prevent wholesale slaughter, has felt obliged to ask the co-operation of the Ambassadors of Turkey's two Allies . . . The position of the Armenians and the system of deportation, dispersion, and extermination that is being carried out against them beggars all description . . . From eye-witnesses in other towns from the interior, I found that the execution of them was everywhere identical. At midnight, the police authorities swooped down on the homes of all Armenians whose names had been put on the proscribed list sent out from Constantinople. The men were at once placed under arrest, and then the houses were searched for papers which might implicate them either in the present revolutionary movement of the Armenians on the frontier or in plots against the Government which the Turks declare exist. In this search, carpets

Avoiding Deportation

The majority of Armenians in the Ottoman Empire were deported, but a limited number escaped this fate. There are several reasons for this. First, many Armenians in areas near the Russian border escaped by fleeing into Russia. In some areas of the Ottoman Empire, Armenians were given the opportunity to convert to Islam as an alternative to deportation. Some took advantage of this opportunity, converting rather than facing almost certain death.

Entire Armenian populations of many villages and towns throughout Turkey were wiped out. However, mass deportations were not carried out in the large cities of Smyrna and Constantinople. The government feared that the numerous foreign diplomats and officials living in these cities would observe such activities, leading to objections and international outrage.

Finally, some Armenians survived because sympathetic Turks, Greeks, and Kurds risked their lives by hiding them from the authorities.

were torn from the floors, draperies stripped from the walls, and even the children turned out of their beds and cradles in order that the mattresses and coverings might be searched.

Not all Ottoman officials went along with the attempt to destroy the Armenians. Some officials refused to comply, including the governors of Aleppo (Syria), Ankara (Turkey), and Kastamonu (Turkey). For their refusal to cooperate, they were dismissed from their positions. Even some higher up in the government objected. For example, Sheik ul Islam, the sultan's representative for religious affairs, did not agree with the plan. A September 14, 1915, article in the *New York Times* noted that Sheik ul Islam was forced to resign because "he disapproved of the extermination of the Christian elements, against which he protested to the Cabinet."

BACKLASH

Deporting Armenians had a negative effect on the health and comfort of the rest of the Turkish population, too. In many towns and villages, a large percentage of the merchants, doctors, lawyers, and craftsmen were Armenians. When they were all deported, there were not enough qualified Turks to take their place. Thus, the local population often experienced a shortage of necessary goods and services. In some areas where most of the farmers were Armenian, there wasn't anyone left to manage the farms, and crops rotted in the fields. In the immediate aftermath of the deportations, a food shortage struck Constantinople because there were not enough workers to harvest food and get it to the city.

EXILE IN THE DESERT

Deportation turned out to be a very effective way of getting rid of the Armenian population. Often, only a few hundred of the thousands of

This 1915 photograph shows men standing among the bones of Armenians who died during the forced marches to the desert during World War I.

deportees in a caravan survived to arrive at their destinations in the desert. Those Armenians who survived to reach Aleppo (a city in northwest Syria) or Deir ez Zor (a city in northeast Syria) arrived starving, barely clothed, and without possessions. Ottoman officials did not allow townspeople, charity workers, and missionaries to feed or assist the deportees. From Aleppo, many were moved south to areas deeper in Syria. A great number of deportees were moved east to the desert near the Euphrates River.

All the places to which the deportees were sent had certain things in common. First, they were inhabited mostly by Muslims, who had completely different cultural and religious habits than the Armenians.

This photograph shows British soldiers in the Mesopotamian (Iraqi) desert during World War I. This harsh, barren region was the final destination of many Armenian deportees.

Second, the locations all consisted of desert or other terrain that made the region physically undesirable. And, finally, they were far away from the deportees' original homes. To make matters worse, the government dumped the deportees in these remote, inhospitable places without supplies, money, or other support. All the able-bodied men had either been killed or impressed into the army or work groups. This left women and children to fend for themselves or perish.

Thousands of Armenians were held in camps in the Euphrates River valley, Syria, and northern Arabia. A February 1917 article in *Current History Magazine*, published by the *New York Times*, provides insight into what life was like in the desert camps. The writer who visited the camps and observed the conditions wrote, "These unfortunate people are penned up in the open like cattle, without shelter, almost no clothing, and irregularly fed with food altogether insufficient."

THE FATE OF CHILDREN

The relocation marches were especially hard on children. Like the adults, many young people were killed outright. Of those who were not killed, many were orphaned. Others had parents taken away to serve the Turks, leaving the children to fend for themselves. Many parentless children were taken in by Greek, Kurdish, or Turkish families and raised with their own children. Sometimes, local women would approach a caravan as it was passing through and offer to take children from their mothers. Authors Donald E. Miller and Lorna Touryan Miller provide an example of just such a scenario. In their book, *Survivors: An Oral History of the Armenian Genocide*, one survivor recounts the experience she had as a child on the march: "About this time, Turkish or Kurdish women would come and take children away," she says. "They approached my mother, too. Realizing that there was nothing but death facing us at that point, she gave me to them."

Other children, however, were not as lucky. They found themselves left completely alone, sleeping wherever they could find shelter and surviving on whatever food they could steal.

After the war, charitable organizations gathered as many of the children as possible, placing them in orphanages and trying to locate their parents. After years of living among people of other ethnic and religious backgrounds, many of the children no longer remembered how to speak Armenian. For those children who had forgotten, special classes were held to teach them about the Armenian language and culture. In many cases, it was not possible to locate relatives of the children. However, a lucky few were eventually reunited with family members.

This photograph from 1915 shows a large number of unfortunate children in an Armenian refugee camp. Many of the children had lost one or both parents.

Thousands of young girls and women were carried off to become servants or wives of Turks or Kurds who attacked the caravans. Certainly, this was a terrible fate to be taken against their will. However, once they became part of the household of a Turk, they were generally safe from further persecution by the government. In Turkish custom, women take their status from the man of the house. So, a woman married to a Turk is considered to be Turkish, no matter what her ethnic background.

After the war, great numbers of young women and girls fled Turkish harems (women's quarters) and households where they were servants, joining the other young people at the orphanages that offered sanctuary for Armenians. In addition, the British carried out house-to-house searches for Armenian women and children who had been taken by the Turks.

RELIEF EFFORTS

The U.S. ambassador to the Ottoman Empire was German-born Henry Morgenthau Sr. In response to the disruption and hardships experienced by Armenians in the Ottoman Empire, he called on his fellow Americans to provide assistance. A number of prominent people involved in religious and charitable work responded. The American Committee for Armenian and Syrian Relief was founded, with Congregational minister James Levi Baron as its head. In 1919, an act of Congress made the organization official and changed its name to Near East Relief. The organization gathered volunteers and money from the Armenian communities in

Above, relief workers distribute bread to desperate Armenians at a refugee center. What little help the Armenians received came mainly from American and European charities.

America and other concerned citizens. Charitable organizations from several European countries also provided aid. Most commonly, these were missionary organizations. They funneled food, money, clothing, and medicine to the displaced Armenians in the Ottoman Empire. In addition, the aid workers were a valuable source of information regarding the plight of the Armenians.

When the Turkish government closed the missionary schools that had served the Armenian community, the people who had been involved with those institutions devoted themselves to trying to help the Armenian refugees. However, their efforts were often halted by the Turkish government. Toward the end of the war, the Ottoman government officials became concerned over the bad publicity that resulted from the reports of the horrible living conditions of Turkish Armenians. They responded by cutting off aid from foreign charitable organizations.

4

The International Community Fails

Ottoman government officials took every step to keep information about their anti-Armenian actions from reaching other countries. They cut off private communication between the capital, Constantinople, and the provinces, as well as between provinces. But they went even further. They censored all mail that left the country, marking out anything they did not want the outside world to see. They even forbade foreign consuls to send telegraphs in code. They searched all travelers leaving Turkey and confiscated written materials. Despite all of these efforts, information about the atrocities leaked out, often reported by missionaries or charitable workers as they returned to Europe and America from Turkey.

REPORTS FROM TURKEY

Government efforts did not succeed in controlling all of the information flowing into and out of Turkey. Letter after letter from missionaries to their parent organizations told of the fate of the deportees. Reports described how deportees were robbed, starved, beaten, and marched away from villages where the missions were located. Others described deportees arriving at the end of the march barely alive. Missionaries were not the only aid workers to send back word of the destruction. As early as March 1915, the Armenian Red Cross fund had reported to the Red Cross in London that conditions were appalling. One hundred twenty thousand Armenians in Armenia had lost everything, and sources in the region reported that the men were being killed and the women carried off.

Another source of information was the press. Both European and American reporters stationed in the area sent stories back to newspapers and magazines. These articles span the time from the start of the massacres, in 1915, through the prosecution of those responsible at the end of the war. For example, the September 24, 1915, issue of the *New York Times* read:

This 1915 photograph shows the difficult living conditions in a refugee camp supported by the American Committee for Relief in the Near East.

500,000 Armenians have been slaughtered or lost their lives as a result of the Turkish deportation order and the resulting war of extinction. Turkish authorities drove the Gregorian Armenians [those of the Armenian Apostolic Church] out of their homes, ordered them to proceed to distant towns in the direction of Baghdad, which could only be reached by crossing long stretches of desert. During the exodus of Armenians across the deserts they have been fallen upon by Kurds and slaughtered, but some of the Armenian women and girls, in considerable numbers, have been carried off into captivity by the Kurds.

INTERNATIONAL RESPONSE

By April 1915, the reports from Turkey clearly indicated that Armenians were being massacred. It was also clear that more atrocities were likely to occur. As Russia was home to a large number of Armenians, the Armenian Church appealed to the Russian government for help. Russia and the Ottoman Empire were on opposite sides in the war, which made it unlikely that the Turkish government would listen to pleas from the Russians directly. They could, however, work with a country not involved in the war. Prior to 1917, the United States was neutral. So, the Russian government asked the United States to try to get the Turks to stop the atrocities being committed against the Turkish Armenians. The U.S. government agreed. Secretary of State William Jennings Bryan sent a telegram to Ambassador Henry Morgenthau Sr., who was stationed in Constantinople. On April 27, 1915, the U.S. government appealed to the Turkish government to take steps to stop the killing of Armenians.

The following day, Ambassador Morgenthau reported back to Secretary Bryan that he and other diplomats in Constantinople were taking up the matter of the massacres with the Ottoman government. The Turkish government, however, was not cooperative. A short time later, it decided to bar foreign aid workers—a move aimed at reducing the number of reports

William Jennings Bryan, U.S. secretary of state at the time of the Armenian genocide, was a lawyer who had unsuccessfully run for president three times before becoming secretary of state.

escaping the area. Turkish government officials told the U.S. State Department that it would not be allowed to send Red Cross doctors or nurses to help the Armenians. In addition, they were barring all other foreigners, including those of neutral countries. Meanwhile, American travelers returning from Turkey in July reported that the deportations of the Armenians were continuing. In response, in October 1915, the United States sent a message through Ambassador Morgenthau to the Turkish government. If the Turks continued to engage in the atrocities against the Armenians, Morgenthau wrote, it would "jeopardize the good feeling of the American people toward Turkey."

German consuls and officials were present in Constantinople and throughout the Ottoman Empire. As the Turks' allies, the Germans were aware of what was happening but did nothing to stop it. Initially, when other countries protested, Germany took the position that it couldn't interfere in the internal affairs of another country. Some countries continued to press Germany, however. In the fall of 1915, for example, the U.S. State Department asked German ambassador Count Von Bernstorff to get his government to intervene on behalf of the Armenians in Turkey. Finally, in response to increasingly bad international publicity, the German embassy in Constantinople filed a protest with the Turkish government regarding the poor treatment of the Armenians.

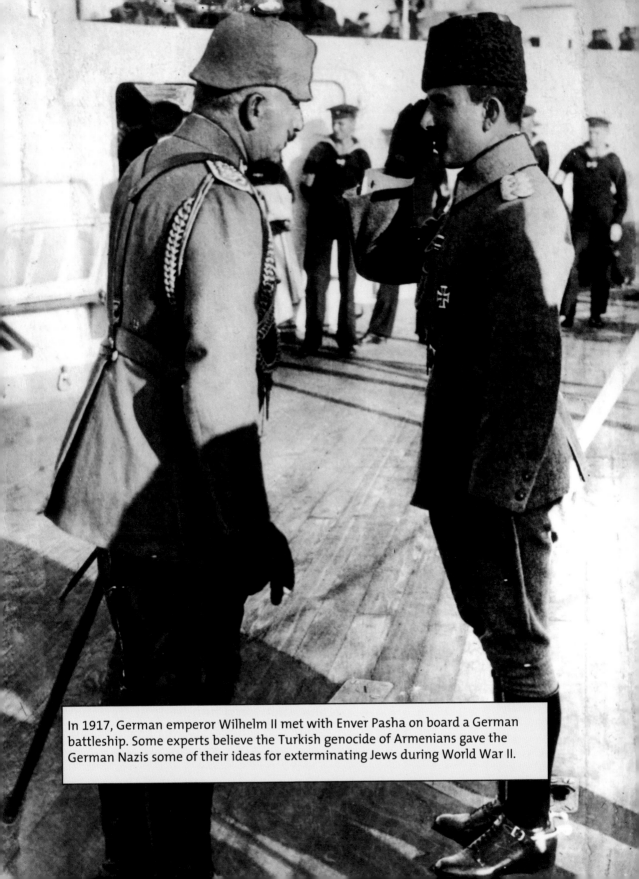

In 1917, German emperor Wilhelm II met with Enver Pasha on board a German battleship. Some experts believe the Turkish genocide of Armenians gave the German Nazis some of their ideas for exterminating Jews during World War II.

On October 6, 1915, Viscount Bryce, former British ambassador to the United States, addressed the British House of Lords (one of the houses of Parliament). He stated that an estimate of 800,000 Armenians killed since May 1915 was quite possible, and that there was "no case of a crime in history so hideous and on so large a scale."

Despite the continued flow of evidence of the Turkish atrocities against the Armenians, the British and American governments did nothing to interfere. Their responses were limited to sending the Turkish government diplomatic protests and requests for a change in behavior. The Turkish government, in turn, ignored them.

According to an article in the *New York Times* published on October 15, 1915, officials of the U.S. government announced that beyond making informal complaints to the Turkish government through Ambassador Morgenthau, they could do nothing further.

The plight of the Armenians continued to affect Americans. On October 18, a committee of prominent private American citizens and well-known Armenians held a protest meeting in the Century Theatre in New York City. The committee was led by Hamilton Holt, editor of the *Independent,* a magazine that had featured many articles about the treatment of the Armenians in Turkey. The committee drafted a series of resolutions, or official judgments, to condemn the actions of the Turkish government regarding the Armenians. While this went on, the Turkish government continued to block foreign aid to the Armenians.

THE END OF THE ROAD

In 1918, the British crushed the Turkish army in the Middle East. Talat, Enver, and Djemal all fled to Berlin, Germany. Others responsible for the deportation and killing of Armenians abandoned their posts, too. As the British advanced into Mesopotamia, they freed hundreds of starving Armenians. The numbers soon swelled to thousands and tens of thousands of hungry, ragged refugees. In Turkey, a new sultan came to

This poster, circulated by the American Committee for Relief in the Near East in 1917, was part of a campaign to help starving and homeless Armenians and Greeks.

power—a mild-mannered man named Mohammed VI. He apologized for the treatment of the Armenians. Later governments would not be so accommodating.

CRIME AND PUNISHMENT

In 1919 and 1920, officials in the postwar Turkish government convened military tribunals to try those responsible for crimes against the Armenians. They believed that Turkey needed to show the world that the country would stand up for justice and human rights. Two of the

Operation Nemesis

Not all Armenians were willing to let the Turkish government, or even international courts, try and punish the Turkish officials who took part in the genocide. Some members of the Armenian Revolutionary Federation were determined to track down and take revenge on the individuals responsible. They were especially determined to find those officials who had gone into hiding after the war. They drew up a blacklist with the names of two hundred people they considered criminals who had organized the genocide. They then set out to assassinate them. This operation was code-named Operation Nemesis. Among those they are said to have killed are:

Mehmed Talat (Talat Pasha), Turkish leader of the CUP, responsible for organizing the genocide; assassinated in Berlin in March 1921

Behbud Khan Javanshir, organizer of Armenian massacres in Baku; assassinated on July 18, 1921, in Constantinople

Bejaeddom Shakir Bey, organizer and executor of the Special Committee; assassinated on April 17, 1922, in Berlin

Jemal Pasha, defense minister; assassinated on July 25, 1922, in Tbilisi, Georgia (one of the countries that used to be part of the Soviet Union)

masterminds of the Armenian genocide, Mehmed Talat and Ismail Enver, had fled the country. Nonetheless, the court tried them in absentia—without their being present. The tribunal convicted Talat and sixteen other leaders for crimes against humanity. Talat, Enver, and Djemal were sentenced to death.

MOVING ON

After the war, some Armenians attempted to return to their home villages. However, most arrived only to find that their homes and property had been claimed by Turks or Kurds, or had been destroyed altogether. In most places, the Armenian businesses, schools, and churches had also

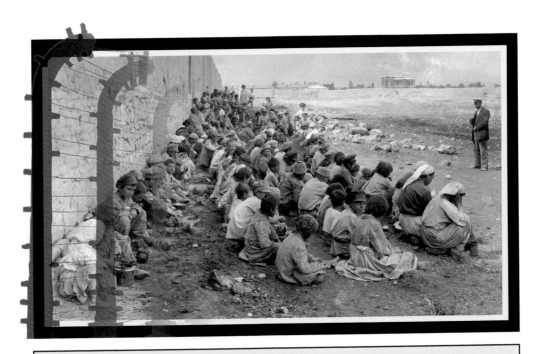

At Marash, Armenia, children of Armenian refugees await daily food distribution by Near East Relief workers. Turks reportedly killed five thousand Armenians in Marash, many of them women and children.

been destroyed. Basically, there was nothing left of their life before the deportations. Furthermore, although many areas were occupied by Entente soldiers, their numbers were not large enough to protect returning Armenians from Turkish retribution. Often, resentful local Turks attacked returning Armenians and burned their homes. Ultimately, the majority of surviving Armenians left Turkey.

5

Armenians Today

Today, some of the largest communities of Armenians can be found in the United States, Russia, France, and Canada. In the United States, large numbers of Armenians live in New York, Massachusetts, and California. In Canada, there are large communities in Toronto and Montreal.

Hundreds of thousands of Armenians fled the Ottoman Empire during and after the genocide. Even more emigrated after the war, looking for a new life in more hospitable lands. A significant number of emigrating Armenians went to America, where they blended into established Armenian communities in New York City and Boston. Many had immigrated to America in the 1890s, after American missionaries had starting going to Turkey. In addition, a growing Turkish carpet industry had brought Armenian immigrants to the United States. By the close of the twentieth century, the number of Armenians in the United States had grown from 100,000 to 800,000.

TURKISH DENIAL

The United Nations has defined genocide as "deliberately attempting to destroy a country or an ethnic, racial, or religious group." The

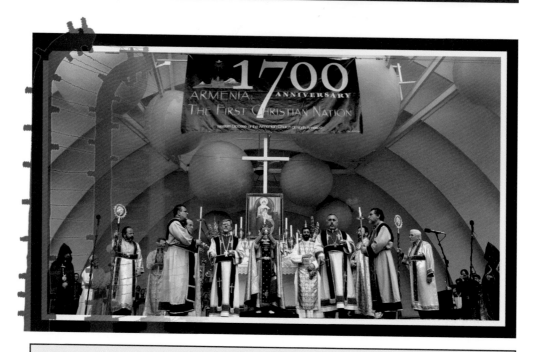

During a 2001 visit to the United States, head of the Armenian Apostolic Church, His Holiness Karekin II, led a ceremony at the Hollywood Bowl. Thousands of Armenians in Southern California attended the liturgy.

destruction can be accomplished either by killing the members of the group or by putting them in a situation where they experience serious harm. Over the years, there has been much debate as to whether Turkey's actions against the Armenians constitute genocide.

The present-day position of the Turkish government is that it did not commit genocide. Instead, it claims it undertook necessary security measures in a time of war. Even at the time, the Turkish government did not deny the atrocities of which it was accused. It simply declared that the measures were necessary to protect the country against possible attack by a disloyal group. The Armenians, the Turkish government maintained, were a rebellious faction, working against the best interests of the empire.

In December 1916, *Current History Magazine* published information from an interview that the Turkish foreign minister, Halil Bey, gave to an Associated Press representative in Vienna, Austria. Halil Bey claimed that the Young Turks had always viewed the Armenians as a valuable asset to the Turkish Empire. However, the Balkan War had led the Armenians to agitate for their own government, separate from Turkey. The Turkish government could not allow this, as the Armenians were not the only people settled in the area they wanted for the Armenian state. Halil Bey claimed that when the war broke out, the Armenians were stockpiling weapons, planning to take advantage of the situation to declare themselves an independent country. He claimed that the only way to stop a nationwide uprising of Armenians was to take drastic measures at the first sign of rebellion. This is largely the position still taken by the Turkish government.

Today, many see the Turkish government's position as not making any sense. If the Ottoman Turks were acting to protect their country in a time of war, why were Armenians deported from all over the empire, even from areas remote from any battlefront? Moreover, why did they deport a vast number of elderly, women, children, and other individuals clearly not engaged in any anti-Turkish military activity?

The question of whether or not genocide occurred has caused difficulties in other countries. In 2006, the French parliament voted to make it a crime to publicly deny the Armenian genocide in France. In response, Turkey cut military ties to France. In 2007, the U.S. Congress was scheduled to vote whether the United States would officially recognize the events that took place as genocide. Armenian communities in the United States had been lobbying hard for the bill. However, the Turkish government was working just as hard to defeat it. The Turkish government warned President George W. Bush that if the bill passed, Turkey might withdraw permission to use bases in its country for sending supplies to U.S. armed forces in Iraq and Afghanistan. Because of this, President Bush pressured Congress to withdraw the bill in 2007. The bill's supporters

Survivors of the Armenian genocide attend a ceremony in Times Square marking the event's ninetieth anniversary. Armenians continue to ask the U.S. government to officially recognize the genocide.

Memorial to the Genocide

In Yerevan, the capital of present-day Armenia, a memorial to the Armenian genocide stands in Tsitsernakaberd Park. The memorial is the result of a demonstration that took place in 1965, when Armenia was still part of the Soviet Union. It was the fiftieth anniversary of the genocide, and for twenty-four hours Armenians demonstrated, demanding that the Soviets officially recognize the genocide. The memorial consists of a central structure as well as a museum and library. The central structure is the Memorial Sanctuary, which is made up of a circle of slabs that are 12 feet (3.65 meters) tall and surround an eternal flame memorializing the victims of the genocide. Nearby, a needle-shaped granite column 145 feet (44 meters) tall points skyward, symbolizing the survival and spiritual rebirth of the Armenian people. The tower is split vertically by a deep crevice. The tower symbolizes both the tragic and violent dispersing of the Armenian people, as well as their unity.

may reintroduce the bill later. Twenty-two countries and forty U.S. states have formally recognized the Armenian genocide.

THE REPUBLIC OF ARMENIA TODAY

At the end of the war, the Ottoman Empire was divided up by the victorious Entente powers. On August 10, 1920, Turkey and the Entente Powers signed the Treaty of Sèvres in Sèvres, France. Unfortunately, there was great objection to the treaty in Turkey. The Turkish National Movement arose. Mustafa Kemal Atatürk wrested power from the sultan and set up a new government, turning Turkey into a republic (a type of government in which citizens elect rulers). In 1920, war broke out between Turkey and Armenia. Armenia lost and was forced to give up

Pictured above is the memorial to the Armenian genocide in Yerevan, the capital of Armenia. The memorial symbolizes the tragic destruction as well as the rebirth of the Armenian people.

much of its territory. At the same time, the Soviet Union invaded Armenia, which collapsed and was then absorbed by the Soviet Union.

In 1991, the Soviet Union broke apart, and on August 23, 1991, the Republic of Armenia declared itself an independent nation. Today, the Republic of Armenia is located between the Black and Caspian Seas. Four countries border it: Turkey to the west, Azerbaijan to the east and south, Iran to the south, and Georgia to the north.

Approximately 3.2 million people live in Armenia. Almost 98 percent are ethnically Armenian. The Republic of Armenia maintains good relations with most countries, including the United States and Russia,

On September 21, 1991, 99.3 percent of the population of Armenia voted to secede from the Soviet Union. Two days later, when the Soviet legislature declared Armenia an independent state, Armenians everywhere celebrated.

although its relations with Turkey are still strained. In contrast to its population of 3.2 million, approximately 8 million Armenians live in other countries around the world, including large communities in the United States and Russia.

TIMELINE

1889 Groups opposed to Sultan Abdul Hamid II come together to form the Young Turks.

1894 Armed clashes pit the Armenian Revolutionary Federation against the Ottoman government forces in Sasun, Turkey.

1906 A branch of the Young Turks forms a political party called the Committee of Union and Progress (CUP).

1909 Armenians in Adana and nearby villages are massacred.

1913 The Teskilati Mahsusa (Special Organization) is placed under the control of Enver Pasha and the Ottoman war department.

August 1914 World War I begins; Turkey joins on the side of the Central Powers; looting of Armenian businesses begins.

December 22, 1914 Enver Pasha, Ottoman minister of war, attacks Russian-occupied Armenia. His forces lose.

1915 The Ottoman government issues an order stating that Christian Armenians must be eliminated; Armenians are killed in towns and villages throughout the empire.

May 27, 1915 The Ottoman government issues the Temporary Law of Deportation, authorizing the transportation of Armenians to remote parts of the empire.

March 29, 1916 The Ottoman government formally rejects foreign aid for deported Armenians.

October 5, 1916 The Ottoman government passes a law that allows it to take ownership of all Armenian real estate.

1917–1918 Entente forces take control of important cities in Mesopotamia (present-day Iraq) and Syria; they start gathering displaced Armenians.

January 19, 1920 The Entente Powers recognize Armenia as an independent nation.

March 14, 1921 Mehmed Talat, leader of the CUP responsible for the Armenian massacres, is assassinated in Berlin by Soghomon Tehlirian, a twenty-four-year-old Armenian.

1919–1920 Under occupation, postwar Turkish government convenes a military tribunal to try those responsible for crimes against Armenians.

November 29, 1920 The Soviet Union invades Armenia, and the country becomes part of the Soviet Union.

1991 The Soviet Union breaks up and the independent Republic of Armenia is formed.

GLOSSARY

Aleppo City in northwest Syria.

Armenian Apostolic Church Christian church to which most Armenians belong.

Armenian Revolutionary Federation Armenian political organization founded in 1890, now an Armenian political party.

atrocity Horrible or monstrous act.

bey Turkish title used by governors and dignitaries.

Central Powers In World War I, Germany, Bulgaria, Austria-Hungary, and Turkey.

Deir ez Zor City in northeast Syria.

deportee Person who is forced to leave a country.

Entente Powers In World War I, Russia, France, Britain, Italy, and the United States; also called the Allies.

genocide Deliberate destruction of one group of people by another.

intellectual Person who engages in mental labor, such as a teacher or writer.

Kurds Tribal people living in parts of present-day Turkey, Syria, Iran, and Iraq.

Mongols Group of Asian tribes originating in Mongolia and China, united by Genghis Khan.

nationalism Devotion to one's own nation.

pasha Title used by Turkish high officials.

plight Unfortunate or difficult position.

proclamation Official government announcement.

propaganda False information spread for the purpose of harming a group.

war profiteer Person who makes large amounts of money by selling scarce supplies during a war.

FOR MORE INFORMATION

Armenian National Committee of America
1711 N Street NW
Washington, DC 20036
(202) 775-1918
Web site: http://www.anca.org/genocide_resource/index.php
The organization maintains records, historic information, quotes, and
    other information related to the Armenian genocide.

Armenian National Institute
1140 19th Street NW, Suite 600
Washington, DC 20036
(202) 383-9009
Web site: http://www.armenian-genocide.org
This organization is devoted to the study of the Armenian genocide and
    offers access to information and photo collections.

Armenian Research Center
University of Michigan-Dearborn
4901 Evergreen Road
Dearborn, MI 48128-1491
(313) 593-5000
Web site: http://www.umd.umich.edu/dept/armenian
The center maintains a database of books, articles, and documents on
    Armenian history and a Web site with useful facts and information.

International Institute for Genocide and Human Rights Studies
255 Duncan Mill Road, Suite 310
Toronto, ON M3B 3H9, Canada

(416) 250-9807

Web site: http://www.genocidestudies.org/Main/Default.htm

The institute promotes the study and publication of information on genocide, including the Armenian genocide.

Project SAVE Armenian Photograph Archives

65 Main Street

Watertown, MA 02471

(617) 923-4542

Web site: http://www.projectsave.org/index.asp

The organization collects, preserves, and presents historic photographs of Armenians and events related to Armenian history.

Society for Armenian Studies

Armenian Studies Program

California State University, Fresno

5245 N. Backer Avenue, PB4

Fresno, CA 93740

(559) 278-2669

Web site: http://armenianstudies.csufresno.edu/sas/

The society promotes the study of Armenian culture and history, and it publishes a newsletter and journal with articles on these areas.

Strassler Center for Holocaust and Genocide Studies

Clark University

950 Main Street

Worcester, MA 01610

(508) 793-7350

Web site: http://www.clarku.edu/departments/holocaust

The center promotes the study of genocide and provides educational programs on the subject.

Zoryan Institute of Canada, Inc.
255 Duncan Mill Road, Suite 310
Toronto, ON M3B 3H9, Canada
(416) 250-9807

Zoryan Institute for Contemporary Armenian Documentation and
Research
2286 Massachusetts Avenue
Cambridge, MA 02148
(617) 497-6713
Web site: http://www.zoryaninstitute.org
The Zoryan Institutes in the United States and Canada work together to
    collect, study, and distribute information on Armenia, its history, and
    its place in world affairs, including the Armenian genocide.

WEB SITES

Due to the changing nature of Internet links, Rosen Publishing has
developed an online list of Web sites related to the subject of this book.
This site is updated regularly. Please use this link to access the list:

http://www.rosenlinks.com/gmt/arge

FOR FURTHER READING

Bagdasarian, Adam. *Forgotten Fire.* New York, NY: Dell Laurel Leaf, 2002.

Balakian, Peter. *Black Dog of Fate: An American Son Uncovers His Armenian Past.* New York, NY: Broadway, 1998.

Kheridian, David. *The Road Home: A True Story of Courage Survival and Hope.* New York, NY: HarperTeen, 1995.

Maybury, Rick J., and Jane A. Williams. *World War I: The Rest of the Story and How It Affects You Today 1870 to 1935.* Placerville, CA: Bluestocking Press, 2003.

Miller, Donald E. *Survivors: An Oral History of the Armenian Genocide.* Berkeley, CA: University of California Press, 1999.

Morgenthau, Henry. *Ambassador Morgenthau's Story.* Detroit, MI: Wayne State University Press, 2003.

Payaslian, Simon. *The History of Armenia.* New York, NY: Palgrave Macmillan, 2007.

Springer, Jane. *Genocide.* Toronto, ON: Groundwork Books, 2007.

BIBLIOGRAPHY

Armenian Weekly. "Anti-Armenian Sentiment Grows in Turkey." Vol. 73, No. 38, September 22, 2007. Retrieved October 6, 2007 (http://www.hairenik.com/armenianweekly/fpg09220703.htm).

Assembly of Turkish American Associations. "Armenian Issue Revisited." Retrieved October 2, 2007 (http://www.ataa.org/reference/facts-ataa.org/reference/facts-ataa.html).

Bryce, Viscount. "The Treatment of Armenians in the Ottoman Empire 1915–1916." HR-Net. Retrieved October 2, 2007 (http://www.hri.org/docs/bryce/appc_toy.htm).

Foreign Policy Association. "War Crimes: Armenian Genocide." Retrieved October 2, 2007 (http://warcrimes.foreignpolicyblogs.com/2007/04/24/the-armenian-genocide).

Hosfeld, Rolf. "The Armenian Massacre and Its Avengers. The Ramifications of the Assassination of Talaat Pasha in Berlin." Internationale Politik. Retrieved October 6, 2007 (http://en.internationalepolitik.de/archiv/2005/fall2005/the-armenian-massacre-and-its-avengers--the-ramifications-of-the-assassination-of-talaat-pasha-in-berlin.html).

Miller, Donald E., and Lorna Touryan Miller. *Survivors: An Oral History of the Armenian Genocide.* Berkeley, CA: University of California Press, 1999.

Missionary Review of the World. "Signs of Death in Turkey." Armenian National Institute. October 1916. Retrieved October 2, 2007 (http://www.armenian-genocide.org/10-16-text.html).

New York Times. "Appeal to Turkey to Stop Massacres. Ambassador Morgenthau Instructed to Make Representations on Request of Russia." Armenian National Institute. April 28, 1915. Retrieved October 2, 2007 (http://www.armenian-genocide.org/4-28-15-text.html).

New York Times. "Armenians Dying in Prison Camps. Hundreds of
Thousands Still in Danger from Turks, Refugee Fund Secretary Says."
Armenian National Institute. August 21, 1916. Retrieved October 2,
2007 (http://www.armenian-genocide.org/8-21-16-text.html).

New York Times. "Defense Committee Corners Supplies." Armenian
National Institute. September 14, 1915. Retrieved October 2, 2007
(http://www.armenian-genocide.org/9-14-15-text.html).

New York Times. "500,000 Armenians Said to Have Perished." The
Genocide Education Project. September 24, 1915. Retrieved
October 6, 2007 (http://www.teachgenocide.org/files/Newsaccounts/
NYT%20Articles/NYT%20 Article%2)-%20Sept%2024,%201915.pdf).

Peterson, Merrill D. *"Starving Armenians": America and the Armenian
Genocide, 1915–1930 and After.* Charlottesville, VA: University of
Virginia Press, 2004.

INDEX

ABOUT THE AUTHOR

Jeri Freedman has a B.A. degree from Harvard University. She is the author of twenty nonfiction books for young adults, and many of them have been published by Rosen Publishing. Her previous titles include *A Primary Source History of the Colony of Massachusetts, America Debates: Civil Liberties and Terrorism, America Debates: Privacy Versus Security,* and *Hillary Rodham Clinton: Portrait of a Leading Democrat.* Freedman lives in Boston.

PHOTO CREDITS